THE LONDON UNDERGROUND
50 THINGS TO SEE & DO

Thanks to Dave Green

- G.M.

This new edition published in the United Kingdom by Duckworth in 2026
First published in the United Kingdom by September Publishing in 2020

Duckworth, an imprint of Duckworth Books Ltd
1 Golden Court, Richmond, TW9 1EU, United Kingdom
www.duckworthbooks.co.uk

Copyright © Geoff Marshall, 2020, 2026

All rights reserved. No part of this publication may be reproduced, stored in a retrieval system, or transmitted, in any form or by any means electronic, mechanical, photocopying, recording or otherwise, without the prior permission of the publisher.

The right of Geoff Marshall to be identified as the Author of this Work has been asserted by him in accordance with the Copyright, Designs and Patents Act 1988.

A catalogue record for this book is available from the British Library

Illustrations by Grace Helmer
Designed by Emily Sear

Printed and bound in China by Xingfa

The authorised representative in the EEA is Easy Access System Europe, Mustamäe tee 50, 10621 Tallinn, Estonia.

1

ISBN: 9780715656563

all the
STATIONS

THE LONDON UNDERGROUND
50 THINGS TO SEE & DO

Geoff Marshall
with Vicki Pipe

DUCKWORTH

CONTENTS

Introduction 9

Historic Underground 10

Stations and Platforms 26

People of the Tube 48

Letter Tube Challenges 52

Unusual Journeys 58

Ticketing and Fares 70

Staircases, Escalators, and Lifts 84

On the Surface 96

Just for Fun 106

Tube Challenges 114

London's Newest Railway 122

50 THINGS TO SEE & DO

1. Ride the Same Route as the First 1863 Tube Train
2. Visit the Transport Museum's Acton Depot
3. Ride the Tube's Oldest Rolling Stock Trains
4. Ride Like Queen Elizabeth II!
5. Take a Train to Ongar
6. Visit All the Tube's Single-Platform Stations
7. Secret Shortcuts at King's Cross Station
8. Shopping on the London Underground!
9. The Busiest Tube Station
10. The Mysterious Middle Platforms at East Finchley
11. Ride a Train on the Wrong Side!
12. Visit an Abandoned Station
13. Who Can You Spot on the Underground?
14. The Z Challenge
15. The R Challenge
16. Ride in Alphabetical Order
17. Ride the 'Secret' Curve of Track
18. The Tube's Strangest Station
19. The Northern Line's Least Used Station
20. The Middle Platforms at Turnham Green
21. Take a Train from Roding Valley to Zone 1
22. Ride the Kennington Loop
23. The Last Remaining Ticket Offices
24. The Tube for Free
25. Buy a Platform Ticket!

CHECKLIST

26	Use a Pink Oyster Pad
27	Off-Peak Treats
28	Bypass the Ticket Barriers
29	Escalator Expedition at Waterloo
30	Lift Off at Greenford Station
31	Walk the Original Fifteen-Storey Staircase
32	How Far Down Can You Go?
33	Secret Staircases
34	Race the Tube
35	Walk Between Covent Garden and Leicester Square
36	The Best Tube Spotting Spot
37	No Man's Land at Southwark
38	Walk the Length of a Tube Line
39	The Victoria Line's Amazing Tile Patterns
40	Under the River Thames
41	The Tube's Longest Journey
42	All Tube Lines Challenge
43	All Rail Lines Challenge
44	The Park Challenge
45	Royal Challenge
46	The Circle Line Challenge
47	Visit All 272 Stations Over a Year
48	The Zone 1 Challenge
49	Visit All 272 Stations in a Day
50	The Elizabeth Line

INTRODUCTION

For thousands of people living in London, the Tube is a mode of transport that's a means to an end. They use it to commute to school and work, they use it to visit friends, they use it go shopping. They'll get on their train, be absorbed in a book, newspaper or more likely their phone, and not engage with the world around them. And then they'll do the same on their return journey as well! This is the world of the Underground, which is often more endured than enjoyed.

But there is another side to the Underground for you to explore – the life of the Tube as you have never known it. There are well-hidden secrets waiting to be discovered, and spaces you may have walked past a hundred times without noticing that there is something to see.

So here you will find historical facts, architectural features, plenty of quirky and unusual things, and more besides. You'll find that the London Underground system can be a place of adventure, a place where railways come to life, and where obscure and unusual things exist – a transport playground!

Here are fifty things for you to see and do while you explore the London Underground. Go have an adventure, Tube Style!

CHAPTER 1

HISTORIC UNDERGROUND

CHAPTER 1: HISTORIC UNDERGROUND

If you were building a brand-new transport system, it would look nothing like the Tube we all know today. This is because it was designed around the city of London, which with its narrow winding streets evolved in a haphazard fashion over a long time.

As the population of London grew, its twisting streets became too busy for everyday life. In 1845, a lawyer named Charles Pearson suggested that an underground railway should be built. He campaigned for its construction over the next fifteen years. Construction eventually started on the first ever Tube line in 1860. Sadly in 1862, only two years later, Pearson died. In 1863, the very first Underground line opened: The Metropolitan Railway.

CHAPTER 1: HISTORIC UNDERGROUND

How Was the London Underground Created?

When the line was built, the underground tunnels followed the paths of the existing streets above. This was the easiest way to construct it. It also meant that the builders didn't have to pay the landowners on the surface any money.

It was originally dug at sub-surface level, which is just six metres underground, and using a method known as 'cut and cover'. The road was cut up, and then the tunnel was dug out before being covered, and the road reinstated. This allowed for a small section to break out into the open and steam to escape; the Underground operated solely with steam trains for the first thirty years. Electric trains didn't come along until the 1890s.

The Underground system was initially built by separate and competing railway companies that didn't always get along. For example, the lines that we know as the Metropolitan line and the District line were owned by two different gentlemen – Edward Watkin on the Metropolitan and James Forbes on the District. They disliked each other immensely and a rivalry formed. Evidence of this can be seen at South Kensington where there are two separate stations. Other examples appear in the different places where lines cross each other but don't connect. (The Piccadilly line crosses the Central line right near Park Royal – it would be very handy if there was an interchange here, but there isn't.)

Now let's go back in time and recreate some of the Underground's historic moments!

CHAPTER 1: HISTORIC UNDERGROUND

Ride the Same Route as the First 1863 Tube Train

Let's start by taking a ride on the Underground and imagining you are one of the first passengers making this trip over 150 years ago.

Where it All Began

Officially, the first part of the Metropolitan line opened for the general public on Saturday, 10 January 1863. Unofficially it had run the day before for officials, staff, and financiers of the railway. The new line included the seven stations between Paddington and Farringdon.

You can do this trip by entering the Circle and Hammersmith & City line station at Paddington and taking a train heading east. When it first opened, it was called Paddington (Bishops Road) station. Not all of the original station names have lasted to the present day. After Bishop's Road, the trains called at Edgware Road, Baker Street, Portland Road, Gower Street, King's Cross, and Farringdon Street.

Nowadays, we know these stations as Paddington, Edgware Road, Baker Street, Great Portland Street, Euston Square, King's Cross St Pancras, and Farringdon. Only Edgware Road and Baker Street have kept their original names.

CHAPTER 1: HISTORIC UNDERGROUND

🔵 Light from Above

At Baker Street it's worth getting out to look at how the station has kept many of its original features. Imagine a steam train putting through here over 150 years ago. Baker Street was built with short platforms. It's the reason why modern-day trains still cannot open the front and last carriage doors when they stop here. See the recesses in the platform walls? This is where natural light used to shine down from the street.

🔵 A 1920s Signal Box

When you reach Edgware Road, there is a signal box on the north side of the station which has only recently been decommissioned. The last lever to switch the train here was pulled in September 2019. From this date onwards, automatic train control was enabled and the signal box was no longer used.

Did you know?

At first there were three trains running every hour (once every twenty minutes), which was then increased to four trains per hour (once every fifteen minutes) during peak hours. The journey time, however, is not all that different from what it is now (around eighteen minutes).

Steam Shafts

At Great Portland Street, there is a gap in the roof at the western end of the station (at the back if you are travelling east). It was built deliberately to allow steam to escape from the underground steam train. Up on the street level, there is a beige-coloured wall, with a street sign, and another sign for the 'International Student House'. It is over this wall that you'll find the gap where steam would have come through many years ago.

The First Hole

Near Euston Square there is a small area of grass – Euston Square Gardens – where the first ever hole was dug to construct the London Underground. Imagine yourself with a shovel, breaking the earth and being the first person to dig the world's first underground railway!

Abandoned Platform

Walk down to King's Cross station and get back on the train heading east. If you keep a sharp eye on the right-hand side, you will see the abandoned platform of the original King's Cross station. Here you'll travel along the long stretch down to Farringdon.

CHAPTER 1: HISTORIC UNDERGROUND

Visit the Transport Museum's Acton Depot

In Covent Garden sits the world-famous London Transport Museum. It is an excellent place to visit for a day out. However, less known is the fact that the Transport Museum has a second place that you can visit – its depot in Acton (nearest station: Acton Town, also on the Piccadilly line). If you like your transport, you will love a day out at the Acton Depot.

What to See

It's called a 'working depot' as there is often work taking place to restore old buses, trains, and other machines that are stored there. You can also see signalling equipment, old signs, engines, artefacts, and an outside storage area with changing displays.

The main attractions inside the depot are the old and restored Tube trains from different years across history. Underground trains are classified by their 'Stock' type, which is either a number or letter that identities what it is, or which line it runs upon. The depot has a 1920s standard stock train here. There is also a 1938 stock train – complete with carriage diagrams from the Northern line at the time. There are also recent modern trains which are no longer in use on the network. A carriage of both A stock (from the Metropolitan line) and C stock (from the Circle line) have been kept here too. Go inside and pretend that you're travelling on an old Underground train.

Best of all there is the Acton Miniature Railway which runs outside, and you can take trips on.

When to Visit

The depot usually has three open weekends per year: one in spring, one in summer, and one in the autumn.

Top Tip!

There are also occasional tours which you have to pre-book on the London Transport Museum website. A volunteer will take you on a tour of the poster store, or objects store, show you transport paraphernalia, and tell the history behind all of them.

CHAPTER 1: HISTORIC UNDERGROUND

Ride the Tube's Oldest Rolling Stock Trains

On the Underground there are different types of trains that run on different lines. Have you ridden on every type of train possible, including the oldest trains that still run on the network?

How Old Are the Tube Trains?

The newest type of train is the 2024 Stock, which was introduced on the Piccadilly line in 2025. They are unique in being nine carriages long – five long car and four shorter cars make up the length of the train. Here are the dates for trains on the other lines:

2010
S Stock trains for the Metropolitan, Hammersmith & City and District lines were introduced between 2010 and 2014. They are seven carriages long, except the Metropolitan trains which have an extra carriage.

2009
The Victoria line trains were introduced in between 2009 and 2011. They are known as the 2009 stock.

CHAPTER 1: HISTORIC UNDERGROUND

1996 — The Jubilee line's trains date back to 1996.

1995 — The Northern line trains date back just a year before, to 1995

1992 — The Waterloo & City line trains are the same as Central line trains (except W & C are only four carriages long while the Central line trains are eight); they both date to 1992.

1973 — The older Piccadilly line trains were built in 1973 and were introduced onto the line between 1975 and 1978. They are still currently in use but are being replaced by the 2024 Stock trains from 2025 onwards. The last of the old trains are expected to be withdrawn in 2028.

1972 — For now, the honour of the oldest trains on the Underground falls to the Bakerloo line with its 1972 trains (the last of which were introduced in 1974). These may be replaced with the 2024 Stock, once the Piccadilly line has received all its new trains!

CHAPTER 1: HISTORIC UNDERGROUND

The Oldest Trains on the Tube

We love the Bakerloo line in winter, there's something cosy, warm and welcoming about it. In the last few years, the trains have been refurbished to have the Barman moquette, the seat pattern you'll recognise across the Underground. This is a standard pattern, but on the Bakerloo line they have their own unique colour. If you've never ridden the length of the Bakerloo line, now is the time do it, because after the new Tube trains are introduced on the Piccadilly line, it is hoped that more will be ordered to replace the aging Bakerloo stock.

There are two other places away from the city where even older London Underground trains run.

Alderney

There is a place where you can still ride an old train from the Tube on the Channel Islands. Most people think of Guernsey and Jersey, but there is also the island of Alderney where a private heritage railway operates on summer weekends and bank holidays. The trains that they use are old London Underground 1959 stock trains, which used to be on the Piccadilly line. They no longer power themselves though, they are just used as carriages. Diesel engines move them up and down the line on this delightful railway, which is two miles in length, with three stops in total.

CHAPTER 1: HISTORIC UNDERGROUND

Isle of Wight

The oldest Underground train in the world which is still in public passenger operation is on the Isle of Wight. Take a trip there and ride the Island Line. The trains here are the 1938 stock Tube trains. These were previously used on the Bakerloo, Piccadilly, and Northern lines. They are suited for the Isle of Wight railway because of the low tunnel at Ryde which they must have clearance on.

Vicki Explores!

If you do go to the Isle of Wight, then you must also visit and explore the Isle of Wight steam railway. You can connect to it at Smallbrook Junction station where the two lines meet. Ride through Havenstreet to Wooton, then back to Havenstreet, where you simply must get out and explore its railway shop, woodland walk, and the children's play area. It's a perfect day out.

CHAPTER 1: HISTORIC UNDERGROUND

Ride Like Queen Elizabeth II!

How many times do you think Queen Elizabeth II rode on the Tube? Once, twice, or maybe never? As far as we know, it's three times! So for some royal fun, why not try to take the same journeys that she has taken.

Trip 1: St James's Park – Embankment – Tottenham Court Road

The first time was in 1939 when she was thirteen years old, and before she became Queen. Elizabeth and her sister, Margaret, were escorted from Buckingham Palace by Lady Helen Grantham (a lady-in-waiting) and their governess, Miss Crawford, to their local station: St James's Park.

They bought twopenny tickets out of the automatic machine and headed to the platform where they boarded a third class smoking carriage so that none of their fellow passengers would recognise them.

They travelled two stops to Embankment and changed onto the Northern line, riding an escalator for the first time. They then travelled to Tottenham Court Road and exited using an escalator again.

CHAPTER 1: HISTORIC UNDERGROUND

Trip 2: Green Park – Oxford Circus

It wasn't until thirty years later in 1969 that Queen Elizabeth rode a Tube train again. To commemorate the Victoria line opening, she took control of a train at Green Park for one stop up to Oxford Circus. As the trains are automatically driven on the Victoria line, she wasn't actually driving the train but merely sitting in its cab!

Trip 3: Hatton Cross – Heathrow 2,3

Queen Elizabeth didn't have to wait another thirty years until she rode the Tube again. This time it was in 1977 – just eight years later – when the Piccadilly line was extended. Up until this point, people travelling to Heathrow Airport could only go as far as Hatton Cross on the Tube, and then they had to get a bus to the airport. But in 1977 the extension was opened, and the Queen was in the cab of the train again as it travelled down to what was then called Heathrow Central. Later it was renamed Heathrow Terminals 1, 2, and 3, and now it's just Terminals 2 and 3 as there is no Terminal 1 anymore.

Did you know?

In 2013, Queen Elizabeth boarded a Metropolitan line train at Baker Street as part of the network's 150th anniversary celebrations, but she did not travel anywhere. It was actually King Charles and Queen Camilla who rode one stop between Farringdon and King's Cross on a Metropolitan line train.

CHAPTER 1: HISTORIC UNDERGROUND

Take a Train to Ongar

There is also another brilliant way to see some old Underground stations, and that's to travel on a private heritage railway.

Where to Go

You can do this up at Epping on the Central line (top right-hand corner of the Tube map) where the Epping to Ongar railway runs. If you look at a modern-day Tube map, you'll see that the Central line ends at Epping, although it once went further to North Weald, Blake Hall, and Ongar. When it was part of the Central line, a shuttle train used to run back and forth to connect with trains that then went all the way into London.

Over time, the amount of people using the line grew fewer, so Blake Hall was the first station to close in 1981. Ticket sales showed that there were fewer than ten passengers using the station per day. The rest of the line was eventually closed in 1994, but the track has remained in place. Ten years later, in 2004, the Epping to Ongar Railway opened as a private company and now runs old trains along the line.

It is not old Tube trains that usually run here, but the trains do travel along the Underground track. Some of the station platforms are decorated with roundels of the names of the stations. There are often steam trains running along here too.

CHAPTER 1: HISTORIC UNDERGROUND

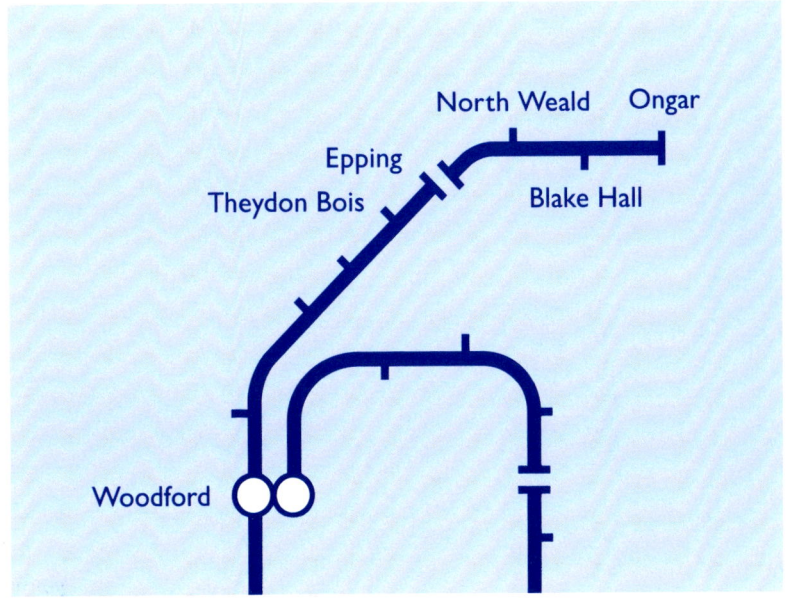

Look out for!

To help staff identify different parts of the track on the London Underground (think of all those in-between spaces!), a project was carried out in the 1970s to measure the tracks in kilometres. Signs were placed at every 100 metres along the way. Ongar was chosen as the zero point on the network – this is the starting point for measurements. There is a marker beyond the buffers which helps you spot the zero point; take a look. In technical manuals today, Ongar is still used by the London Underground for measurements even though the station has been closed since 1994!

//
CHAPTER 2

STATIONS AND PLATFORMS

CHAPTER 2: STATIONS AND PLATFORMS

A lot of Tube stations are laid out in a standard two-platform configuration with one train going one way and another train going the other way.

But where two or more lines converge are stations that are called an interchange: they are designed to have different levels so the Tube lines do not intersect. These are often in Zone 1 (in the middle of the Tube map). They are not simple stations. They have complicated corridors, stairs, and escalator systems, but with plenty of signs telling you which way to go. This means you can often have an adventure just by walking around a station and exploring everything that there is to see.

CHAPTER 2: STATIONS AND PLATFORMS

Visit All the Tube's Single-Platform Stations

6

How many Underground stations do you think have a single platform? Have a guess!

Ok, so the answer is four. The four stations that a have single platform are Chesham on the Metropolitan line, Mill Hill East on the Northern line, Kensington (Olympia) on the District line, and Heathrow Terminal 4 on the Piccadilly line. Can you visit them all?

Chesham on the Metropolitan line is slightly awkward because it's so far away from London. In fact, it's not in London at all but in the county of Buckinghamshire. When you get there, you'll see evidence that it used to be a much bigger station. There is an abandoned platform and an old water tower (from the days of steam trains) that is no longer in use. The building is still here, and it has the lovely feel of a small station that is far, far away from the hustle and bustle of central London.

🟦 Mill Hill East is another station which feels a long way from London, but it's comfortably inside Zone 4. The line used to be part of an old steam railway that ran all the way to Edgware. In the 1930s, the line was electrified as far as Mill Hill East, but as the Second World War broke out the work stopped and was then never finished. After the war, passenger usage fell, and when the Underground took over the station they only kept it running as far as the electrified section. Here you can walk along the footpath of the line where the steam trains used to run all the way to Edgware.

🟦 Kensington (Olympia) is an intriguing one. The station as a whole doesn't have one platform, it has three. Only one of them is used exclusively by Underground trains (as part of the District line) while the other two platforms are used for London Overground and National Rail services. Olympia gets a very limited service during the week with quite a sparse service at weekends. It's not an easy station to visit and tick off the to-do list!

🟦 Heathrow Terminal 4 is the busiest of all the single-platform stations as thousands of people travel through the airport every day. What we like about Heathrow Terminal 4 is that it's the only station on the Underground network where trains travel in one direction only (clockwise) around the airport loop. When trains arrive here, there is a scheduled stop of five to ten minutes, which allows time for the driver to get a cup of tea and go to the toilet. The service then starts again and takes the train back towards central London.

CHAPTER 2: STATIONS AND PLATFORMS

Secret Shortcuts at King's Cross Station

King's Cross St Pancras is a complicated 'hub' station in Zone 1 and it serves the busy mainline station up above. It is also where three deep-level lines (Victoria, Northern, and Piccadilly) and three sub-surface lines (Metropolitan, Hammersmith & City, and Circle) all meet, connect, and interchange.

In order to keep people moving around the station, signs are deliberately placed in a way that steers you a very, very long way around when changing lines. This is done to stop everyone taking all the shortcuts.

Victoria Line to Piccadilly Line

If you are changing from the Victoria to the Piccadilly line – at the front of the train (heading south) or back of the train (heading north) – take the exit that is at that end of the platform. This leads you into an area where you will see three escalators ahead that take you up to the main exit. However, look just to the right and there is a sneaky little passageway with some steps. Follow them down and they will take you to an area where the Piccadilly line stretches on your immediate right. This is the quickest way to get to it from the Victoria line, and vice versa if you're coming the other way.

Piccadilly Line to Northern Line

There's also a sneaky interchange corridor that is not used very much between the Piccadilly and Northern line. From either Piccadilly line platform, use the rear exit for northbound trains, or front exit for southbound trains. Here the space opens into an entrance with some steps down to a passageway. This bends to the left and takes you down some more stairs then brings you out onto the southbound Northern line platform. It's the quickest way to change between these two lines.

Victoria Line to Street Level

Now to our favourite shortcut, which will take you to a place that you've never seen before. This is the fastest way out of the Victoria line to street level. On the platform of the Victoria line, follow the sign that says 'Exit to Pentonville Road'. Walk down a yellow corridor to an area where there is an escalator up to street level. It's fast because so few people use this route and you can speed through.

Don't forget to admire the incredible mosaic on the wall in the ticketing area, complete with a roundel and double arrow National Rail symbol.

CHAPTER 2: STATIONS AND PLATFORMS

Shopping on the London Underground!

There used to be a time when Underground stations and platforms had many shops. But did you know the Underground also famously had pubs? Liverpool Street and Sloane Square were two such locations, but those days are long gone. However, there are still some places where you can buy a snack.

Central Line

🟦 **Epping:** newspaper kiosk on Platform 2. It's only open until eleven a.m.

🟦 **Woodford:** a fabulous kiosk that sells snacks and makes an excellent cup of tea. Located on the southbound/London-bound platform.

Metropolitan Line

🟦 **Amersham:** a newspaper kiosk on the southbound platform that sells drinks and snacks.

🟦 **Pinner:** a small kiosk on the southbound platform that is only open in the mornings.

🟦 **Baker Street:** there's a newsagents on the northbound Metropolitan line platforms, as well as several shops inside the ticketing area within the gateline (barriers).

CHAPTER 2: STATIONS AND PLATFORMS

Circle Line

🟦 **Embankment:** bizarrely there are FOUR newsagents' kiosks on the platforms here. We don't know why they need so many, but you could go and buy something from each one to say that you've done all four.

🟦 **Sloane Square:** the location where the pub used to be on the westbound platform is now a small kiosk for snacks and drinks.

🟦 **Westminster:** there is a popular high street coffee shop on both the westbound and eastbound platforms here.

🟦 **Liverpool Street:** a kiosk on the sub-surface eastbound.

District Line

🟦 **Southfields:** there's a kiosk at the bottom of the stairs as you come onto the platforms.

🟦 **Chiswick Park:** a tea and coffee kiosk sits inside the gateline at the bottom of the stairs that lead up to the westbound platform. We've never actually seen it open, but that may be because it's only open early in the morning and we've never been there at that time.

🟦 **Upminster:** there's a Coffee Link kiosk on the London-bound platform of the C2C trains, but it still counts as it's inside the gateline at an Underground station.

🟦 **Barking:** several kiosks across all the platforms of this National Rail station.

🟦 **Richmond:** (again on the National Rail platform but still counts!) there's a sweet shop and coffee shop.

🟦 **Ealing Broadway:** (also on the Central line) three outlets serving food and snacks on the interchange passage between the two lines.

🟦 **Wimbledon:** a Snax shop immediately inside the gateline before you go down the stairs. There are a whole range of other outlets on the concourse right before you get to the trains.

District & Piccadilly Lines

🟦 **Hammersmith:** there is a newsagent on both of its platforms.

🟦 **Acton Town:** a newsagent on the westbound platform.

Jubilee Line

🟦 **Stratford:** a mega-hub of a station with plenty of shops (and a huge shopping centre!) outside. This has led to many kiosks and coffee shops springing up inside the station's gateline too.

Waterloo & City Line

🟦 **Bank:** a tiny little kiosk is squeezed between the two platforms at the Bank terminus. Buy a snack and then hop on the train for a four-minute ride!

CHAPTER 2: STATIONS AND PLATFORMS

Ghost Kiosks

These are the many places that used to serve up snacks on the Underground, but not anymore …

See if you can spot the marks where a square-shaped kiosk used to sit at Gloucester Road on Platforms 1 & 2.

At High Street Kensington, on Platform 2, there used to be a newspaper kiosk at the front of the platform. If you were standing at the right door, it would have once been possible to hop off the train, buy a newspaper, and hop back on again just as the doors were closing. All in just the twenty seconds that it stopped on the platform!

There is another lovely ghost kiosk on the westbound platform at St James's Park. It used to be a news stand selling papers and magazines. The wooden shell is likely to be one of those features you've walked right past without even realising.

CHAPTER 2: STATIONS AND PLATFORMS

The Busiest Tube Station

You will often hear that Oxford Circus is the busiest station in the Tube network, considering it's a station that just has Underground services. In actual fact, the Tube's busiest station is Bank. That's counting all the people who enter and exit, AND all the people who pass through to use it as an interchange station.

Bank was given its name because the Bank of England is located on the surface above. The station opened in 1884 as part of Monument station. The two stations are known as the Bank Monument complex and are so close together that commuters can access both by walking between them underground.

Bank station was recently redeveloped with a new entrance that opened in 2024, which amusingly is on *Cannon Street*, but also just a thirty second walk from one of the entrances to *Monument* Tube station, making it the shortest distance between entrances of two different stations on the network.

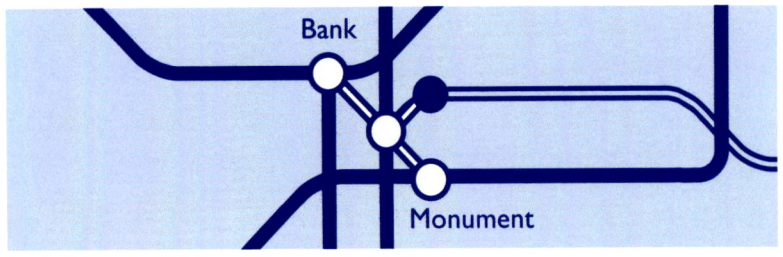

CHAPTER 2: STATIONS AND PLATFORMS

Vicki Explores!

While you're at Bank, take a look at the brilliant statue just outside, by exit/entrance number 3.

This is a statue of James Henry Greathead, the pioneer of the tunnelling shield. A tunnelling shield is a protective structure used during the digging of tunnels. It acts as a support structure to prevent the soft earth from collapsing in on those working on the tunnel. Greathead was the first person to build a patented cylindrical shield. The shield was also used to dig the Tower Subway, a passenger walkway that went under the River Thames near Tower Bridge.

If you look closely at the statue of Greathead, down to his feet on the base of the plinth, you'll notice a grille of a few centimetres deep that runs all the way around. This is a ventilation point from somewhere down below. Here air is escaping out of the tunnels that Greathead helped to dig, and into the fresh air above!

Remember! Bank station is one of the busiest stations, so make sure you visit in off-peak hours or at the weekend to avoid the commuter traffic.

CHAPTER 2: STATIONS AND PLATFORMS

Take a Trip Around Bank Station

Did you know it is possible to walk around the corridors of Bank station and not repeat yourself, while staying underground for fifteen minutes? Here's how to do it:

Step 1 Start at the Central line ticket hall, enter any of the main numbered entrances that are in a circle on street level. You can then walk around in a complete circle at this point, coming back on yourself before going to the gateline.

Step 2 Next go down the escalators and turn right to walk along the Central line's westbound platform until you see the sign for the Northern line. This will take you down a spiral staircase and into a corridor which leads to an open area with a spot for buskers. Go down the steps towards the Northern line platforms. Here you can walk along the new widened southbound platform opened in 2022.

Step 3 At the end, turn left and follow the signs for a small corridor which is signposted for the DLR. Follow this and you'll go down some narrow steps and a narrow corridor which takes you to the DLR platforms.

CHAPTER 2: STATIONS AND PLATFORMS

Step 4 Don't get on the DLR! Instead, follow the signs for the Central line, which will take you up and onto the escalator. Keep going straight, go up another escalator, and when you get to the top turn left, following signs for the Waterloo & City line.

Step 5 This is the long corridor that takes you under the red tunnelling shield still embedded in the wall. It was used in the construction of the Waterloo & City line in the 1890s.

Step 6 Before you get to the Waterloo & City platform, you'll see the new way in and out of Bank Tube station – the Walbrook Street entrance.

Step 7 Do this without repeating yourself by using the steps or lift. At the top, turn around and use the escalators to come down again. At the halfway mark you can admire the backlit artwork that depicts the Roman heritage of the site.

Step 8 Head down to the Waterloo & City line platforms, and now you get to ride the travellator – which is quite exciting – that will then take you back up to the Central line ticket hall. Now that's a walk which should take you at least fifteen minutes to complete!

CHAPTER 2: STATIONS AND PLATFORMS

The Mysterious Middle Platforms at East Finchley

If you've ever hopped on or off at East Finchley on the Northern line, you'll notice that it has two island platforms, and four tracks in total. Almost all the trains that stop here do so on the outside, Platforms 1 and 4. So what about Platforms 2 and 3 in the middle?

Well, they do get used but only when trains are coming out of a depot, or sidings, and are entering service. Or at the end of a day when a southbound train from High Barnet terminates there before heading off to the depot for the night.

There are ten trains in the morning between 5 a.m. and 7 a.m. that enter service on Platform 2 before heading north to High Barnet. In the evening after 11 p.m., there are eight trains which have travelled south from High Barnet to terminate for the night at East Finchley and come in on Platform 3.

CHAPTER 2: STATIONS AND PLATFORMS

Stylish Station

The station is gorgeous. It's a rebuilt 1930s Art Deco station conceived by the renowned Tube architect Charles Holden. It has beautiful semi-circular glazed stairways which lead to a footbridge. At the other end of the platform is a glazed window area that is used as a passenger waiting area.

Rare Station Statue

Here there is a famous statue by British Sculptor Eric Aumonier called 'The Archer'. You can only see it upon entering the station at the start of your journey.

The sculpture was unveiled in 1940 and was described as 'more than a decorative device; it is powerful symbolism'.

It still is. The archer's bow follows the line of the railway, and points towards the entrance of the longest tunnel on the Underground. This stretch of railway enters seventeen miles of tunnel, along the length of the Northern line, which finally opens out at Morden.

CHAPTER 2: STATIONS AND PLATFORMS

Ride a Train on the Wrong Side!

Trains come out of the depot and into service at the start of the day, or go back to the depot at the end of the night. This is when a lot of 'irregular' train moves happen.

White City to Central London

At White City, westbound trains depart from Platform 1, while eastbound trains depart from Platform 4. In the middle is Platform 2, a platform where some trains from central London terminate. On the other side is Platform 3, where trains depart again heading eastbound.

Except! There's an anomaly: the last westbound train on the Central line. It leaves from the middle platform, rather than the regular westbound platform (Platform 1). The obscure thing to do here is get the last train out of White City that heads west from the eastbound platform.

CHAPTER 2: STATIONS AND PLATFORMS

 Running Right

White City is just one of six stations where the trains are right-hand running. So, instead of passing on the left (as you would do on the road), the trains here run on the 'wrong side' of each other. The other locations that have right-hand running trains are Warren Street, Euston, and King's Cross on the Victoria line, as well as Bank and London Bridge on the Northern line.

Central Line to Ealing Broadway

Here's an unusual one we discovered accidentally when travelling early one Sunday morning. If you are travelling west on the Central line to Ealing Broadway, it's possible to get there by getting on a train at West Ruislip. You then change at North Acton and walk over the footbridge to what is normally one of the two eastbound platforms. From here, a train arriving from West Ruislip then heads out west and not towards Ealing Broadway. It's a very unusual train movement.

We can only find one instance of this happening on a Sunday morning, and at no other time. It's a tricky one to do!

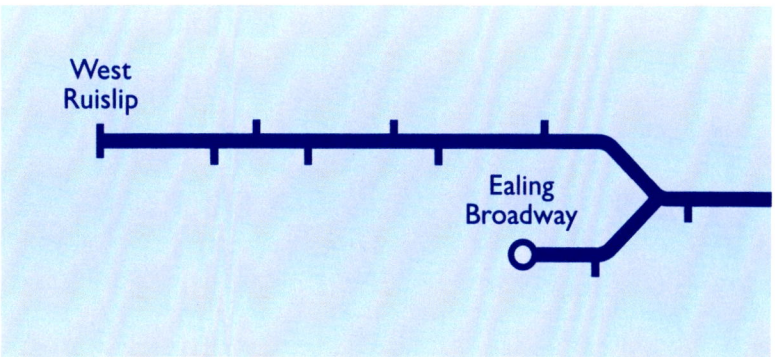

CHAPTER 2: STATIONS AND PLATFORMS

Visit an Abandoned Station

How many disused and abandoned stations are there on the Underground? It's a tricky question.

The answer is not as simple as you might think. Some stations that used to exist on the network have been completely removed. There is no longer any trace of them. There are other stations that have unused platforms underground but no building on the surface, and there are those which do still have a surface building.

What about a station that was moved slightly from one location to another? There are places where parts of the original station still exist, but with a new station close by. There are also stations which belonged to the London Underground network, but have now been taken over by National Rail stations – so the station isn't closed at all, it's still served by trains, just not Tube trains; complicated, isn't it?

Taking all of these possibilities into consideration, the agreed number of abandoned and disused stations is forty-nine, and it's always exciting to go and visit one.

CHAPTER 2: STATIONS AND PLATFORMS

How to Spot an Abandoned Station

A simple way to see an abandoned station is to visit sites where there is still a surface building. For example, Aldwych or Brompton Road on the Piccadilly line, and South Kentish Town on the Northern line are places where you can walk right up to the gorgeous red-tiled buildings, touch them, and take a picture of yourself in front of them.

In some places, you can see the abandoned platforms from a passing train as you whizz by them. This includes Osterley & Spring Grove on the Piccadilly line, and the original King's Cross on the Metropolitan and Circle lines.

● Station Tours

If you truly want to get inside, you have to take an organised tour. These sometimes have an age restriction and do not allow children under fourteen to take part so finding the buildings on the surface or spotting them as you pass by on a train are fun alternatives for a family day out.

CHAPTER 2: STATIONS AND PLATFORMS

Abandoned Stations to Spot on the Surface

▪ South Kentish Town is on the Northern line between Camden Town and Kentish Town. Walk along Kentish Town Road, the main road, then at the junction with Castle Road you'll see the red-tiled building which was once a station.

▪ York Road was on the Piccadilly line between King's Cross and Caledonian Road. Walk up York Way from King's Cross; when you get to Bingfield Street, look out for the old station building on the surface.

▪ Marlborough Road was on the Metropolitan line, and now stands as a white-painted building on the junction of Finchley Road and Queen's Grove. It's just a short walk north from St John's Wood station on the Jubilee line.

▪ Fulham Broadway was rebuilt a few years ago, with a new entrance which is part of a shopping centre. The original station building still stands as 'Market Hall'. You can go inside and see the old ticket hall windows, or outside at the side of the building you can peer through a gate to see some old steps that used to go down to the platform.

CHAPTER 2: STATIONS AND PLATFORMS

Abandoned Stations to Spot from a Train

🟦 Down Street is on the Piccadilly line in between Green Park and Hyde Park Corner. The point at which the platforms have been bricked up provides the evidence. You can spot the tunnel wall changing to bricks as the train goes past. If you're heading west from Green Park, or east from Hyde Park Corner, always look out the right-hand side of the train (facing direction of travel).

🟦 Osterley & Spring Grove is just 200 metres east of the current-day Osterley station, and the old platforms are still in place. If you are travelling to or from Osterley station, look out of the windows (best done during daylight!) to spot the original station.

🟦 King's Cross is a short distance east of the current station. If you're on a train heading east towards Farringdon, look out of the window on the right-hand side and you'll see the old section of platform still in place that used to be the original station.

CHAPTER 3

PEOPLE OF THE TUBE

CHAPTER 3: PEOPLE OF THE TUBE

Who Can You Spot on the Underground?

We've seen a lot of stations, many lifts and escalators and station signs, and we've ridden a lot of trains. There is, however, another important aspect to the Underground that makes it work, and that is the staff that work on it! So next time you're out and about, say 'Hello!' to some of the people that work there, ask them how their day is, and chat to them about their job! Here's some of the people you can meet …

CHAPTER 3: PEOPLE OF THE TUBE

🔵 Train Operators

The most obvious job that might spring to mind are train drivers, although in the world of the London Underground the official title that they use is train operator. You may also see it abbreviated down to the letters TO.

Extensive training takes place for train operators, with many hours spent on extremely life-like simulators which have been placed at each line's depots. Trainee train operators work their way up and go out on the rails with an instructor operator. After sixteen weeks of training they are allowed to drive Tube trains by themselves.

- -

🔵 Platform Staff

Sometimes people are recruited directly onto a training programme, but it's more than likely that train operators have worked their way up from other roles. Platform staff and gateline staff have the tough job of dealing with members of the public. If trains are late or delayed, it's the staff on the frontline that have to respond to customers face to face.

Platform staff also help with ticketing in the ticket halls. As staffed ticket offices were all closed, there are staff out in the ticket areas to help passengers with queries and the use of ticket machines. They've also got handy tablet devices which allow them to look up information and deal with more complicated queries.

CHAPTER 3: PEOPLE OF THE TUBE

● Revenue Inspectors

If you don't have a ticket you will be in trouble if you are stopped by a revenue inspector! They lie in wait at stations and monitor people coming through ticket barriers to check that people aren't dodging the fares. They have access to the CCTV system so they can go back and review footage to see if someone is a persistent offender or not.

● Train Presentation Crews

The train presentation crews are the brilliant teams who pick up the litter and keep your trains clean. The most likely place that you'll spot them is at the end of lines, where the trains sit for a few moments before they go back out again. They use this time to pick up discarded litter and newspapers.

● Line Controllers & Signallers

Signallers make sure that trains are going to the right places and are on time. Line controllers keep a wider eye on the service and train patterns. They respond and react to incidents that may occur if something goes wrong. On the Central line, for example, line controllers and signallers work in a control centre that is based at Wood Lane (White City) to monitor the state of the network.

CHAPTER 4
LETTER TUBE CHALLENGES

CHAPTER 4: LETTER TUBE CHALLENGES

Pick up a pocket-sized Tube map at any station. It shows you the classic map of the London Underground (along with London Overground, DLR, TfL Rail, and Tram services) which you are familiar with.

Now turn it over onto the other side; there is an alphabetical list of all the stations (with a grid reference so you can look up where they are on the map). This is just what you need to refer to in this chapter. Here we'll be having some fun with challenges based on the names of the stations and the letters that are in them.

CHAPTER 4: LETTER TUBE CHALLENGES

The Z Challenge

Do you know the only station on the Tube map that has got the letter Z in it? Have a think! And while you do, consider visiting twenty-two stations in alphabetical order.

Why only twenty-two when the alphabet has twenty-six letters? Look at the index on the back of a Tube map. There are no Underground stations that start with the letters J, X, Y, or Z. There are only twenty-two letters of the alphabet you can go through with the Tube stations.

A fun thing to do is to visit twenty-two stations in alphabetical order. You can start at a station that begins with A and finish your route with a station the begins with a W. For example: Angel, then Bank, then Chancery Lane … and so on, until you get to a station that starts with the letter W.

Once you've done that, you could visit the only station with the letter Z in it, which is Belsize Park on the Northern line.

(If you really wanted to do the missing letters, then St James's Park could work as a J, you could do Hatton Cross for the X, and Belsize Park for the Z! We're still not sure about the letter Y though!)

CHAPTER 4: LETTER TUBE CHALLENGES

The R Challenge

Here's a delightful piece of trivia which turns itself into a journey you'll want to make.

If you take the Metropolitan line from Amersham all the way down to Liverpool Street (on an Aldgate-bound train), you stop at twenty-two stations in a row that all have the letter R in. Like this:

AmeRsham, Chalfont & LatimeR, ChoRleywood, Rickmansworth, MooR PaRk, NoRthwood, NoRthwood Hills, PinneR, NoRth HaRRow, HaRRow-on-the-Hill, NoRthwick PaRk, PReston Road, Wembley PaRk, Finchley Road, BakeR StReet, GReat PoRtland StReet, Euston SquaRe, King's CRoss St PancRas, FaRRingdon, BaRbican, MooRgate and LiveRpool StReet.

It's just Aldgate that doesn't play ball! If only it were called Aldersgate …

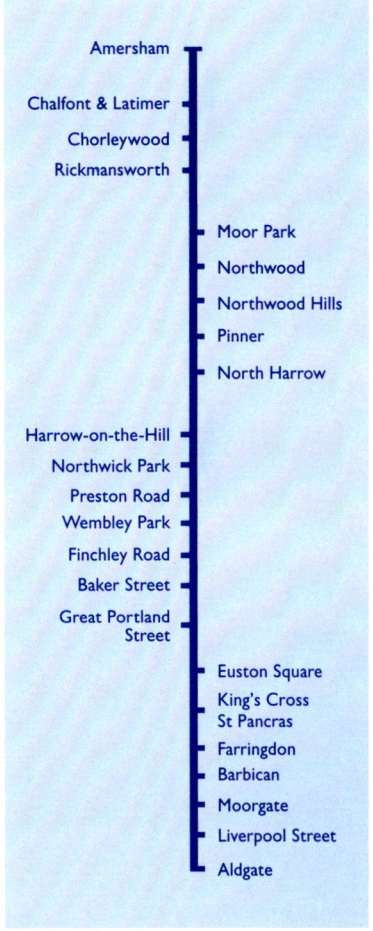

CHAPTER 4: LETTER TUBE CHALLENGES

Ride in Alphabetical Order

More fun can be had with the alphabet and Underground station names. Try to ride through different stations in alphabetical order. Unfortunately, there are no routes which go directly up the alphabet, so no stations beginning with A then carrying on to B, then C, and so on. Instead the game here is to find stations which run up the alphabet so that no matter how far apart the letters are, at least the alphabetical ordering is correct. We think there are seven places on the Tube where you can get five stations in a row. Can you ride them all?

We can't find anywhere on the Tube map, using only Underground stations, where this works for more than five letters. There is however one that works on the Overground to give you a six!

Canonbury, Dalston Junction, Haggerston, Hoxton, Shoreditch High Street, and Whitechapel.

CHAPTER 4: LETTER TUBE CHALLENGES

First up, on the Piccadilly line start your journey at Arsenal and head north. You will travel to Finsbury Park, Manor House, Turnpike Lane, and Wood Green. That's A, F, M, T, and W to give you your five consecutive letters.

On the Hammersmith & City line you can travel from Baker Street to Edgware Road, Paddington, Royal Oak, and Westbourne Park, giving you B, E, P, R, and W.

On the District line there is Barons Court, Hammersmith, Ravenscourt Park, Stamford Brook, and Turnham Green, that's B, H, R, S, and T.

Over on the Jubilee line it's possible to journey through Bermondsey, London Bridge, Southwark, Waterloo, and Westminster to get five letters, B, L, S, Wa, and We.

Next is the Northern line with Borough, Elephant & Castle, Kennington, Oval, and Stockwell, which is B, E, K, O, and S.

And finally, the Metropolitan line has two places where you can get five in a row. They are:

Croxley, Moor Park, Northwood, Northwood Hills, and Pinner; and Eastcote, Rayners Lane, South Harrow, Sudbury Hill, and Sudbury Town.

CHAPTER 5

UNUSUAL JOURNEYS

CHAPTER 5: UNUSUAL JOURNEYS

When you think of the Underground, the Tube map is likely to be the first thing that comes to mind. It is a brilliant diagram which simplifies the network. It can be used at a glance, as quickly as possible, to make journeys on the network easy to navigate.

But there are some quirks in the network that the map doesn't necessarily show: curves of track where services run, sections of lines where limited services run, and train services that even start out as one line then change halfway through into another.

Here are some secret journeys for you to take, which aren't obvious just from looking at the map!

CHAPTER 5: UNUSUAL JOURNEYS

Ride the 'Secret' Curve of Track

It's not common that a service isn't shown on the official Tube map, but that's exactly what's happening in the top left-hand corner of the Metropolitan line.

Where is It?

A short curve of double track called The North Curve exists between Rickmansworth and Croxley on the Metropolitan line. Usually, only empty trains use this piece of track. At the start of the day and at the end of the day trains need to be in the right position. At Rickmansworth there are sidings – low-speed track sections – where a train will come out, run empty, and slowly run over the curve, under a bridge (where a footpath through the woods lies above), and then pick up its first passengers at Watford as it begins its service.

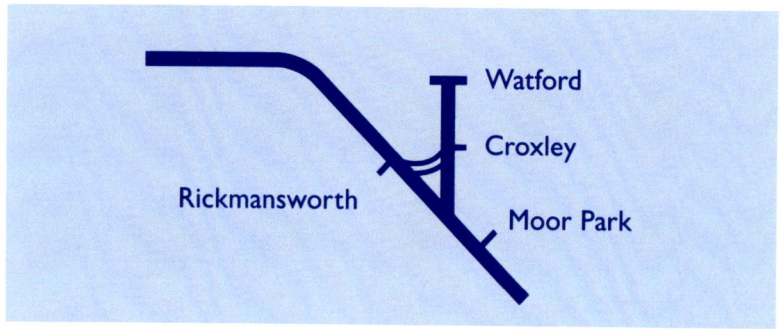

CHAPTER 5: UNUSUAL JOURNEYS

How to Ride It

There are usually two passenger services a day on this curve of track, in the morning and evening. At 5.15 a.m., the first train of the day departing from Chesham travels over this curve after Rickmansworth and travels up to Watford. Later in the evening at about 12.45 a.m., a train leaving Watford heads south and rather than going to Moor Park, it travels along the north curve and goes to Rickmansworth instead.

Sometimes there is a more regular service due to engineering works (usually at a weekend) when the line is closed at Moor Park and all trains out of Amersham or Chesham go back and forth over the curve to Watford. There are also special rail tours that take you on the Metropolitan line and which travel on the curve.

Vicki Explores!

There's a fun walk that you can also do near here. Take the Tube to Croxley, and then walk down the road to Croxley Green, turning onto All Saints Lane. This takes you into the woods of Boundary Walk. Keep walking along the path until you reach the footpath which goes over a bridge. Here is a crossing over the North Curve and the Metropolitan line. You can get a great view down onto the tracks below.

CHAPTER 5: UNUSUAL JOURNEYS

The Tube's Strangest Station

One of the best strange stations on the Tube's network is Kensington (Olympia). It's a National Rail station with an additional small, single platform for Underground trains.

Why is it So Strange?

When the London Overground started four services per hour here in December 2011, the regular District line trains from Mondays to Fridays were cut right back (the regular weekend service is unaffected). There are now a small number of departures from Olympia very early in the morning, and then two in the evening that run from High Street Kensington to Olympia.

Hidden Platforms

The best part about this odd service are the two rarely used platforms at High Street Kensington. Platform 3 is the one that's used the most (but infrequently!) to facilitate this service, while Platform 4 is tucked away and poorly signposted down a narrow staircase. It is hardly used at all. These platforms are worth exploring on their own. You can see where a tunnel's construction was started, heading north towards Notting Hill Gate. There's already one tunnel and two tracks here, so the plan was for two tunnels and four tracks in total, but it was never completed.

CHAPTER 5: UNUSUAL JOURNEYS

The Northern Line's Least Used Station

Mill Hill East is the Northern line's least used station, and a fun train to ride because of its odd scheduling.

During the day, and at weekends, the trains that run to Mill Hill East simply shuttle back and forth every fifteen minutes to Finchley Central. But it is possible to get a direct train from Mill Hill East that isn't the shuttle but goes directly into central London. Have you ever done it?

In the morning, the Northern line trains start at Highgate Sidings, call at East Finchley and Finchley Central, and then run to Mill Hill East. From the first train up until 9.30 a.m., they form services that run directly into central London and don't simply shuttle back and forth.

The shuttle then operates between 9.30 a.m. through until 4.45 p.m., after which the trains going to and from Mill Hill East run to central London. This happens until around 7 p.m., at which point they switch back to be a shuttle service again.

CHAPTER 5: UNUSUAL JOURNEYS

The Middle Platforms at Turnham Green

Turnham Green in Chiswick is predominantly a District line station. The configuration of the station means there are two island platforms with the District line running on the outside. In the middle, the Piccadilly line trains pass without stopping on the fast tracks. Except for early mornings and late at night! That's when the Piccadilly line does stop here – before 6.45 in the morning, and after 10.30 in the evening – to allow for better connections with the District line to Richmond.

Why Does this Happen?

In 2014, Transport for London (TfL) ran a consultation with thousands of local residents suggesting that the Piccadilly line would stop (when new trains were introduced). But it was decided that this would not happen as it would add too much time on to the route. The service pattern remains the same with Piccadilly line trains stopping here only in the early morning and late evening when the line is less busy.

The stopping pattern incidentally does include night Tube services, and since it began in August 2016 Piccadilly line trains stop at Turnham Green on Friday and Saturday nights. So … can you get on or off a Piccadilly line train at Turnham Green?

A Meeting of Two Lines

The only other times you might see a Piccadilly line train stopping here are under two rare circumstances. The first is when engineering works are taking place on the Piccadilly line tracks, but the District line tracks are unaffected. Piccadilly line trains often run along the District lines instead and stop at Turnham Green. Or (as has happened to me!) due to an incident on the Piccadilly line (but not the District), a Piccadilly line train may get held at a red signal and if line control informs the driver that they will be held here for a while, they can let passengers out onto the platform to continue their journey on a District line train.

Did you know?

In 1913, the Central London Railway (Central line) obtained parliamentary permission to extend the line to Richmond. This would have meant the construction of a deep-level station at Turnham Green. The stations each side would have been at Heathfield Terrace and Emlyn Road. The plan was delayed by the First World War and an alternative route was adopted in 1920, so it never happened.

CHAPTER 5: UNUSUAL JOURNEYS

Take a Train from Roding Valley to Zone 1

21

The Hainault Loop at the eastern end of the Central line has always been a lesser-used part of the London Underground. It was previously run with steam trains before it became part of the Underground in the 1940s. Over the years it has been used as a testing area for automatic trains. Victoria line trains were tested here back in the 1960s, and the service has never been that frequent either.

Vicki Explores

Take a ten-minute walk from the station to see a great piece of architecture. Turn right as you exit, go down Station Way to the main road called Buckhurst Way. Turn left onto this and then almost immediately there is a sideroad on the right called Hornbeam Road. Go down here, then follow the sign for the Air Cadets Club, which will lead you to a large field. Cross this field and onto the footpath which takes you down to the Roding river and you'll discover a small viaduct which Central line trains rumble over.

CHAPTER 5: UNUSUAL JOURNEYS

A Rare Service

Up until the 1990s there were no trains after 8 p.m., and even nowadays trains are only once every twenty minutes during off-peak hours (more frequently during peak hours). Only the branch to Chesham on the Metropolitan line has a less frequent service.

And since January 2020, due to upgrade works taking place to Central line trains, there are now just two trains that shuttle back and forth between Hainault and Woodford.

The Trains that Keep Going

Because of a nearby Central line depot at Hainault, a small number of trains go straight through to central London. On a weekday there are just three trains, between 6.30 and 8 a.m., that carry on after Woodford and go to West Ruislip. On Saturday mornings there are two trains, and on Sunday there is just one service, which leaves Woodford, goes to Hainault and then carries on through to Ealing Broadway. Can you catch one of these trains?

Top Tip

At the station, there is a timetable poster showing the train times. What you're looking for are the times that are coloured in red. Note that this works at Chigwell and Grange Hill stations as well, but we like doing it at Roding Valley because, in terms of yearly passenger numbers, it is the least used Underground station.

CHAPTER 5: UNUSUAL JOURNEYS

Ride the Kennington Loop

Have you ever wondered why the Northern line splits and has two branches as it goes through the centre of London? The answer is simply because the two branches were originally two separate railway lines, built by two separate railway companies. For operational purposes, today it is treated as two separate lines that just happen to have the same name and colour on the Tube map. The Charing Cross branch typically runs services between Kennington and Edgware, and the Bank branch typically runs between Morden and High Barnet.

The Birth of the Northern Line

What is known as the Bank branch today was initially built by, and called, the City & South London Railway. It ran from Stockwell in south London up through London Bridge and the City, terminating at Euston. What we now know as the Charing Cross branch was a separate line known as the Hampstead Tube. Its full name was the Charing Cross, Euston & Hampstead Railway.

In the 1920s both of these lines were extended, and then connected at Camden in north London, as well as Kennington down in south London. Around the same time, competing railway companies started to merge together, and these two separate branches became one to form the Northern line.

Loop-the-Loop

At Kennington (where southbound trains from Edgware terminate) there's a brilliant thing to do. You can be on a train that departs from Kennington, and a few minutes later … it arrives at Kennington!

Once the southbound Charing Cross train terminates, it leaves the station heading south. Then it enters a loop of track that dips down under the line heading south to Morden before turning north. The train then comes back into Kennington station on one of the two northbound platforms; it's usually an empty train, ready to run up to Edgware. It's therefore possible to ride the train that goes around the Kennington loop by staying on when everyone else gets off. It takes about five minutes (and the train may stop) to travel around. If you look down through the train to the other carriages, you'll be able to see it sharply curving. You'll then arrive back at Kennington, heading north!

Remember, not all Northern line trains terminate at Kennington when heading south. When heading north it's common for most northbound trains to head up the Bank branch towards High Barnet.

X and Y Decoded

In signalling terms, the Charing Cross branch is labelled X (for Cross) and then Y is used for the Bank branch because it follows on from the letter X. The signallers refer to both lines as the X and Y branches.

CHAPTER 6

TICKETING AND FARES

CHAPTER 6: TICKETING AND FARES

The London Underground has had many types of ticketing arrangements throughout its history. Originally, paper tickets were bought on a 'point to point' basis, similar to the ticket for a National Rail service, alongside return and season tickets.

Travel zones were first introduced in London in 1981 along with a ticket known as the Capital Card, which later transformed into the Travelcard. In 1991, these travel zones changed into the six principal zones that are still used today. (Zones 7, 8, and 9 are now used further out, but Greater London is covered by Zones 1 to 6.)

Originally, there were ticket inspectors at every station who you would show your ticket to, but automatic gates were introduced to the system in the 1960s.

CHAPTER 6: TICKETING AND FARES

Tickets Today

The Oyster cards that we use widely today were introduced by TfL in 2003, and since then they have brought in contactless card payments, where adults can now just tap in with their bank card, or smartphone, to pay for travel.

There is speculation that Oyster cards may not be around for ever. However, under 18s use the Zip Oyster, and there are still those who have Railcard products (which cannot be linked to a contactless bank card) so it is likely that Oyster will be here for some time yet.

As the Oyster scheme has grown all over London, it now also incorporates other rail travel, such as National Rail and the DLR. The system behind it has become extremely complex, but includes a daily cap, which is a set price for travelling through different zones. Once you have made multiple journeys, you will hit the cap price and won't pay for any more journeys for the rest of the day.

There are now several anomalies in the system that you can try – let's do some of them!

CHAPTER 6: TICKETING AND FARES

The Last Remaining Ticket Offices

Most London Underground stations lost their ticket offices in 2015. But there are still some Tube stations that have them, which means you can still buy a physical ticket. As you can no longer pay for a bus journey using cash, the day may come when it is the same for travel on the Underground, so buy a paper ticket now as a souvenir before the chance is gone.

District line: Wimbledon, Barking, Upminster

Bakerloo Line: Willesden Junction

London Overground: Queen's Park, Kensal Green, Willesden Junction, Harlesden, Stonebridge Park, Wembley Central, North Wembley, South Kenton, Kenton, Harrow & Wealdstone, Richmond

Remember! Buying a paper ticket for the Tube always costs more money (sometimes double!) than using an Oyster card. TfL deliberately make paper tickets more expensive in their continual drive to get everyone to switch over to Oyster or contactless technology.

CHAPTER 6: TICKETING AND FARES

The Tube for Free

Would you like to ride the Tube for free? Well then, you'll need to know about the Heathrow Free Travel Zone!

An arrangement between TfL and the airport allows passengers to change between terminals without paying anything. If you're arriving on one flight into one terminal and need to connect to another terminal for another flight, you can do it without paying anything for the connection. This means there is free travel on Tube trains between four stations: Heathrow Terminal 5, Terminals 2 & 3, Terminal 4, and Hatton Cross.

Travel Tip

The free travel zone also applies to buses that connect between the terminals, so if you want to take a free ride on a bus, you can do so. All the buses that connect between the hotels and the terminals are free too.

CHAPTER 6: TICKETING AND FARES

Where to Go

You can touch in and out at any of the three Heathrow terminal stations, and you won't get charged anything – you can also change at Hatton Cross, but only a change there; if you get out you will be charged! Therefore, the journeys you can do for free are:

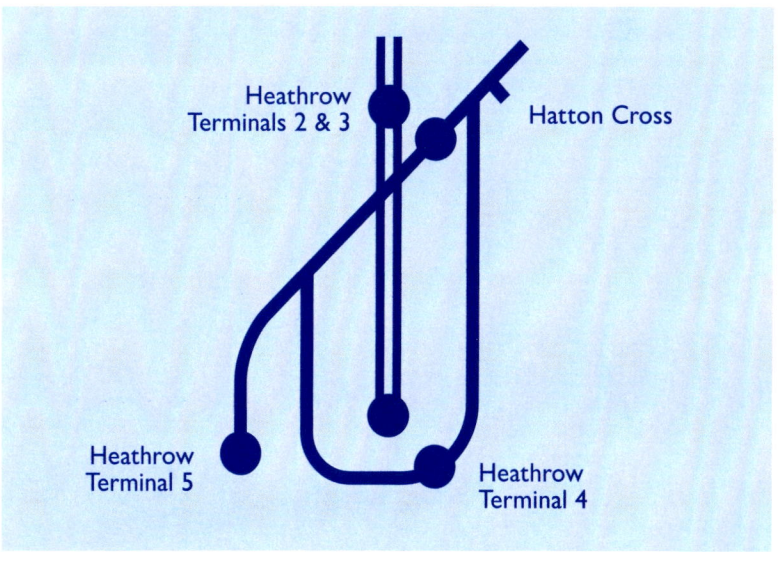

- Heathrow Terminal 5 to Terminals 2 & 3
- Heathrow Terminal 5, change at Hatton Cross to Terminal 4
- Heathrow Terminals 2 & 3, change at Hatton Cross to Terminal 4
- Heathrow Terminal 4 to Terminals 2 & 3
- Heathrow Terminal 4, change at Terminals 2 & 3 to Terminal 5

CHAPTER 6: TICKETING AND FARES

Buy a Platform Ticket!

The notion of a platform ticket seems like a quaint novelty from a bygone era. It was a ticket that was available at large mainline railway stations. For a small fee, it would let you into the station, but not onto the train. This would be used, perhaps, to wave a family member off or by train enthusiasts who wanted to spot trains from the platform, but not go anywhere. The unusual thing that you may not know is that it's still possible to buy one for the Underground from a ticket machine.

How to Buy a Platform Ticket

1. At a station, go up to the full-sized ticket machine and select 'By Destination' on the main screen.

2. It will then ask you to type in your destination. Type in the letters 'P' and 'L' and it will throw up the stations Plaistow and Plumstead as destination ... but look!

3. Listed in between is also 'Platform Ticket'. Select it.

4. The ticket costs one pound to buy.

5. A paper ticket with that station's name on it will print out.

6. It is valid for an hour to spend on the platform of that station.

7. The ticket quite clearly states 'NOT FOR TRAVEL' so please do remember you can't use it to travel on a train.

Travel Tip

An interesting place to use this is in the area of no man's land at Southwark station connecting to Waterloo East station – more on this area later.

CHAPTER 6: TICKETING AND FARES

Use a Pink Oyster Pad

Oyster pads are all over London and are used by the Underground, National Rail, the DLR, Tram, and buses too. They allow you to touch your Oyster card on them to tap in and tap out of your journey. On the Underground system, Oyster pads are yellow, but have you ever noticed that there are some pink ones too?

The reason they exist is because TfL charge more for journeys that go through the Zone 1 area. But in some cases, it's possible to avoid travelling through Zone 1 between two stations. If you take a slower or indirect way, and you change trains during your journey, you need to tap on the pink Oyster pad to prove that you've gone that way.

There are sixteen locations that have pink Oyster pads:

CHAPTER 6: TICKETING AND FARES

Blackhorse Road ....

Canada Water ....

Clapham Junction ....

Gospel Oak ....

Gunnersbury..............................

Hackney Central/Downs ....

Highbury & Islington ....

Kensington (Olympia) ....

Rayners Lane ....

Richmond ....

Stratford ....

Surrey Quays ....

West Brompton ....

Whitechapel ....

Willesden Junction ....

Wimbledon ....

Heathrow Airport to Upminster (avoiding Zone 1)

This one is our favourite journey to do this, and we challenge you to do it too by tapping in at the appropriate times.

Start at Heathrow Terminal 5, and catch a Piccadilly line train to Acton Town.

At Acton Town change to the District line and travel to Turnham Green.

Change again at Turnham Green and go down one stop to Gunnersbury.

On the platform at Gunnersbury there is a pink Oyster pad; touch your card on it.

Then catch an Overground line train through to Gospel Oak. There is a pink Oyster pad there too which you need to tap onto.

Catch a train from Gospel Oak all the way to Barking.

At Barking change onto the District line and travel up to Upminster.

Don't forget to tap out!

In doing so, you have travelled from Zone 6 in west London to Zone 6 in east London, without going through Zone 1. Touching on two pink Oyster pads proves that you've travelled an indirect route.

CHAPTER 6: TICKETING AND FARES

Off-Peak Treats

Travelling is broken down into peak and off-peak fares, for both adult (18+) and child (11 to 17) fares.

TfL Peak Times: journeys that are started in this time are charged at a higher rate.

MORNINGS	EVENINGS
6.30 a.m. to 9.30 a.m.	4 p.m. to 7 p.m.

However, here's the brilliant thing: the peak times aren't those exact times! There are a few minutes of grace to allow you to touch in a moment early and catch a train at 9.30 a.m. So here are the actual times:

> In the morning, the peak period starts at 6.35 and ends at 9.27.

> In the evening, the actual times are 4.05 and 6.57, when it finishes.

CHAPTER 6: TICKETING AND FARES

Bypass the Ticket Barriers

There are a small number of entrances where it's possible to enter or exit without going through a ticket barrier. Instead, there are Oyster validators. You must still touch in or out, but there's no physical barrier preventing you from entering or exiting the stations. Remember, you must still touch in and out at these stations.

The stations that do not have ticket barriers are:

Finsbury Park (via National Rail)

Waterloo (Waterloo & City)

Buckhurst Hill

West Finchley

Epping

Chalfont & Latimer
on the northbound platform, side entrance.

Chorleywood
on the northbound entrance/exit.

Finchley Central
on the entrance/exit to the station.

Mill Hill East
it's the Northern line's least used station, so no real surprise that there are no barriers here.

Pinner
on the northbound platform (towards the back of the train) there are steps down to an ungated entrance/exit.

Roding Valley
the least used station on the entire Underground has no barriers on either of its two entrances.

South Kenton
at the Bakerloo line's least used station, there's no space to install barriers.

West Harrow
on the westbound entrance/exit to the street.

Woodside Park
on the northbound side of this station.

CHAPTER 7

STAIRCASES, ESCALATORS, AND LIFTS

Of course, to get to London Underground's trains you have to travel down beneath our feet to get to the platforms.

This was initially done with just steps, then lifts. Escalators came along later, which helped move higher numbers of passengers more quickly. It's a complex world of passenger transportation through different depths underground.

Escalator Expedition at Waterloo

According to TfL's official figures, Bank has the most escalators with thirty-five, and Waterloo comes next with twenty-six. But there are four *travelators* at Bank and two at Waterloo, which are not escalators but moving walkways, which means that Bank has a total of thirty-one, while Waterloo is in second place at twenty-four.

Challenge 9 takes you around Bank, so here you can take a walk around Waterloo and ride on all its escalators! Like this …

CHAPTER 7: STAIRCASES, ESCALATORS, AND LIFTS

How to Use All Twenty-Four Escalators at Once!

Step 1: On the National Rail concourse there are three escalators that take you down to the ticket hall for the Bakerloo and Northern lines. They're quite short in length but always busy, especially at peak time. Ride these three first, by going down one, then up one, and down the other!

Step 2: From the ticketing area, go through the gateline and go left, and there are three escalators here that go down to the Bakerloo line. You can go down one, up another and down another again! That's six done.

Step 3: Once at the bottom, there are two more escalators on the other side of the wall. We have to admit that these are tricky because they're only open at peak hours. In the morning they're both set to come down, then they're switched off during the day until the evening peak hours when they're switched on again to whisk people up from the Tube. Do these two next, and you've done eight!

Step 4: Back in the ticket hall, you can now head for the Northern line. There are three escalators that go between the gatelines, down to the area with steps that lead to the Northern line platforms. Again you'll probably find yourself going down one, then up one, then down one again, at which point you are eleven escalators complete!

Step 5: Ok, the next three are part of a recently refurbished entrance called the South Bank entrance, and there are three shiny new escalators here. You'll need to go up one, down another, and up the other to take your total to fourteen. Then come back down one of them (but don't count it).

Step 6: To finish up, follow the signs and head over for the Jubilee line. To get there you'll find yourself encountering the travellator! If you've never done this before in both directions then now is clearly the time to do it. These don't count towards the escalator total, they're just fun to do.

Step 7: Ok! Now back in the area that takes you to the Jubilee line, there are two sets of three escalators that take you down to the platforms. Go down one, up another, and down the other. Then walk the length to the other end of the platform and the other set of escalators, which you go up, down a different one, and then up again to come back to where you were a few moments ago. You're twenty escalators complete!

Step 8: The last four are then right here: two sets of two going up, and two going down, which take you to and from the Jubilee line ticket hall. Ride all four, finish at the top in the Jubilee line ticket hall and you are done! All twenty-four escalators complete.

Did you know?

All escalators on the Tube are numbered. On the escalator there is a fairly big number in black, stamped onto the top and bottom ends so that they can be identified individually.

CHAPTER 7: STAIRCASES, ESCALATORS, AND LIFTS

Lift Off at Greenford Station

In November 1987, a terrible accident occurred at King's Cross station when a fire broke out. The flames burned up underneath a wooden escalator coming from the Piccadilly line and caused many deaths. From the inquiry that followed, it was determined that a discarded match, that was still lit, had been dropped on the escalator to cause the disaster.

After the report was published, new fire regulations were subsequently brought in and all wooden escalators were replaced with metal ones. All the ones that were actually underground that is. The ones in the open were still wooden, which is why, for several years, there was a wooden escalator at Greenford station which was seen as an oddity. It became the last surviving wooden escalator on the Tube. Greenford station train tracks run high above street level, so it was also one of the few places where you would take an escalator up to platform level rather than down.

In 2015 the wooden escalator was taken out and replaced with an incline lift, a first for the Underground! These are lifts that travel sideways as well as up and down on an angle. It brought step-free access to the station.

Top Tip

There are now five other incline lifts in London. Four are on the Elizabeth line (at Farringdon and Liverpool Street stations) and the other is down by the River Thames on the north side of the Millennium Bridge. St Paul's is the nearest station. Once you've ticked off going on the incline lift at Greenford, go and do the others as well.

Did you know?

It is well known that the longest escalators on the Underground are at Angel on the Northern line. Lesser known are the locations for the shortest escalators. These are the two that are at Stratford station and take you up from either the Jubilee line or the ticketing area to the Central line level.

CHAPTER 7: STAIRCASES, ESCALATORS, AND LIFTS

Walk the Original Fifteen-Storey Staircase

31

Plenty of stations in the central area of the Underground – Zone 1 – were built with just lifts and an emergency spiral staircase. Many of these stations have been upgraded to have escalators. These can carry many more people and are much faster than stairs and lifts. For some stations in the Zone 1 area, it's not possible to install escalators because there's no space to do so. Regent's Park on the Bakerloo line is one of these – although it is underused compared to one of the Tube's more popular stations: Covent Garden.

Stepping Up

When you do get to Covent Garden, it's busy during peak times and you often have to queue to get into the lift here, which is why many people take the stairs. There are 193 steps on the spiral staircase at Covent Garden. Officially, posters and announcements try to dissuade you from using them. It's quite a slog and you do need to be fit. Famously, there is a sign clearly stating that the 193 steps are 'the equivalent to a fifteen-storey building', and therein lies an amusing tale …

It seems that the station's poster is used in a few other places. You can see it at Russell Square (which has 175 steps) and Hampstead (which has 320 steps). Tottenham Court Road used to be the same too with its old spiral staircase, which is sadly now gone and no longer accessible after the ticket hall was completely rebuilt in 2016 for the new Elizabeth line. But if Covent Garden had 193 steps and Russell Square and Hampstead have a different amount, they can't all be fifteen-storeys high!

So How Many Storeys High Are These Staircases?

Well, it can vary depending on the measurement of the steps involved. On average we go by the calculation that there are sixteen steps per floor. So Covent Garden is the equivalent of climbing a twelve-storey building, Russell Square is eleven, but Hampstead (the deepest station on the network) is the same as a twenty-storey building!

Did you know?

A lesser-known fact about Covent Garden is that it was also considered for closure back in the 1930s. When the line was extended at either end – to speed up journey times through the centre of town – York Road, Down Street, and Brompton Road stations were all closed. These are three of the seven disused Tube stations on the Piccadilly line. Covent Garden was also considered for closure, but this never happened, thankfully!

CHAPTER 7: STAIRCASES, ESCALATORS, AND LIFTS

How Far Down Can You Go?

Here's another one of those great Tube trivia questions: 'what is the deepest station on the London Underground?' It can also be phrased as 'what is the deepest part of the Underground?'

The answer is not as straightforward as you might think because the deepest section of tunnelling beneath sea level is on the Northern line between Waterloo and Kennington. Here it is twenty metres underground. But the deepest Tube station is at Hampstead where the platforms are fifty-eight metres below ground level, because it's on a steep hill. It also has the deepest lift shaft on the whole network at fifty-five metres tall, and the deepest emergency staircase.

CHAPTER 7: STAIRCASES, ESCALATORS, AND LIFTS

Down Below

Legend has is that the station supervisor's room at Hampstead station has a logbook. Over the years, on their first day, members of staff are told to go and walk the staircase. The supervisor times and records how long it takes the new member of staff. The logbook is said to go back several years with many walking times listed.

And that's where you come in! Fancy some exercise? You do have to be relatively fit to do this one, but the fun part is timing yourself doing it. It can take about seven to eight minutes to walk up the entire spiral staircase at Hampstead station.

Once you're at the top, why not go down again? If you can't face the stairs, take the lift (which is obviously the longest lift journey on the Underground as it goes to the deepest platforms).

The Forgotten Station

There's one final thing to tell you here. Hampstead almost wasn't the deepest station! To the north lies the half-built station of North End. It acquired the nickname 'Bull & Bush', which is the name of a local pub.

The station was never finished due to opposition from Hampstead locals and people who accessed the nearby Heath. The remains of the construction still exist as an access point today. From The Old Bull & Bush pub, head a little north, then turn right into Hampstead Way. On the bend in the road you will see a building on the left which is behind a fence and locked gate. A sign there says: 'Keep clear. Exit from emergency escape route'. It uses the tell-tale font which is the Johnston Underground font. This leads down to the Northern line below.

CHAPTER 7: STAIRCASES, ESCALATORS, AND LIFTS

Secret Staircases

What are the most complicated stations on the Underground? It's likely that your answer would be King's Cross, Euston, Westminster, or Waterloo, which are indeed a complex mass of tunnels, stairs, and escalators.

But one incredibly complicated station that often gets overlooked is Embankment. Here the sub-surface lines for the District and Circle lines meet the deep-level lines of the Northern and Bakerloo lines. A whole warren of passageways link everything together. It's in here you'll find the most secret of staircases, unused by passengers!

Where to Find It

Inside Embankment station, find the place where an escalator goes down to the northbound Northern line. Just to the right of this is an unsigned corridor, which takes you down to a staircase. It's a spiral staircase that no one ever goes down. At the bottom, it brings you out to another short corridor which will be empty. At the end is a beautiful, long, green-tiled corridor which leads down to one of the Northern line platforms.

CHAPTER 7: STAIRCASES, ESCALATORS, AND LIFTS

🔵 Moorgate

At Moorgate station, rather than going down the escalators to the Northern line, there is a short corridor to the right that leads you to a spiral staircase. Again, it feels as though hardly anyone ever goes down there. Halfway down, you will get to the platform for the Great Northern line trains (not part of the Underground), which definitely has a disused feel about it. Carry on down the stairs, and it will bring you to the end of the northbound Northern line platform.

🔵 Bank

At Bank station, follow the signs and find the lifts that take you from the Northern line up to the ticket office. There are three lifts here but there was space for a fourth. The space is now used by a modern-day staircase, which is square in shape, instead of the traditional spiral.

🔵 Shepherd's Bush

Can you find another staircase that is not spiral in design? At Shepherd's Bush, on the Central line, there is one tucked away which is quite hidden. You can find it down a corridor which leads off to the right at the bottom of the escalators.

CHAPTER 8
ON THE SURFACE

CHAPTER 8: ON THE SURFACE

Having explored the stations, walked stairs, and taken lifts and escalators, let's turn our attention to the numerous places where the Tube is above ground. On the surface, they may not be so hidden, but can still exist in unusual places that you wouldn't expect. The best thing about this section is that the things to do are free. Let's look at some things you can do with the Tube up on the surface and don't involve having to pay for a ticket.

CHAPTER 8: ON THE SURFACE

Race the Tube

In 2014, a popular video called Race the Tube showed someone get off a Circle line train at Mansion House, exit the station, and run down the road in ninety seconds to then get back onto the same train at Cannon Street. It took that team several attempts before it worked, and they had people on the surface wearing hi-vis jackets to act as lookouts for traffic in order to allow the runner to run safely.

We cannot recommend running between two stations, but there is another intriguing possibility that you can do: walk between two stations faster than a train.

CHAPTER 8: ON THE SURFACE

How to Do it

Option one

The eastern part of the Circle line, heading towards Aldgate, is the place to do it. It's perfectly possible to get out at one of the earlier stations, and walk south along the streets through London, until you get to another station.

The first one to try is on the Circle line between Barbican station and Mansion House. Up on the surface, you turn right out of Barbican, go past the large roundabout by the Museum of London, turn left past St Paul's station on the Central line, and then turn right down Bread Street, taking you down to the junction where Mansion House is. This trip normally takes fifteen minutes by train but should be walkable in twelve to thirteen minutes. Arrange to meet a Tube-travelling friend outside Mansion House station and see who can get there first.

Option two

It should be possible to achieve the same trick on the Circle line between Farringdon and Blackfriars. Again, leave a friend on a Circle line train that's going clockwise around the circle and see if you can walk to Blackfriars quicker than they can get there. While they're going the long way around via Aldgate (which will take about twenty minutes) you can walk by foot. Go down Farringdon Street, heading towards the River Thames, and you'll reach Blackfriars station.

Finally, we should say that it might also be possible to repeat this trick between Moorgate and Cannon Street, but for that you do need to be a fast walker as the timings are a lot tighter. It could be possible.

CHAPTER 8: ON THE SURFACE

Walk Between Covent Garden and Leicester Square

35

Did you know that the distance between Leicester Square and Covent Garden is the shortest distance between two Tube stations? Actually, yes, you probably did, as it is one of the most common facts that comes up when discussing the Underground.

At just 250 metres apart, the two Piccadilly line platforms are exceedingly close. The train typically takes just thirty-five to forty seconds to travel between them. Which is why it can be quicker to get out at Leicester Square and walk.

If you're already on the Piccadilly line then don't do this, but if you're travelling on the Northern line, with the intent of changing at Leicester Square onto the Piccadilly line, then it is always quicker to exit the station here, take a short walk along Long Acre, and reach the outside of Covent Garden in a quicker time.

Why not try it out? Go with a friend, have one of you exit at Leicester Square and do the walk. The other can go along the corridor, wait for a train, make the short journey, but then contend with having to wait for a lift at Covent Garden station, and then exit.

CHAPTER 8: ON THE SURFACE

The Best Tube Spotting Spot

For this next trip, you need to jump on the District line and head towards Putney. Go south, down from Earl's Court, and then after Putney Bridge look out of the left-hand side of the window to see the bridge over the Thames and people walking alongside it.

To get to the bridge, travel to East Putney station, exit left out of the station, and then turn right into Oxford Road. Go down Merivale Road, turn right, and you'll see a railway bridge, and at this point some steps that lead up to it.

This takes you to a brilliant and secret part of London, Fulham Railway Bridge, which is a railway bridge with a footpath along the side (not a road bridge). You can walk alongside the District line here watching the trains as they clatter their way across the river.

Stop halfway across, take a photo, or even take a selfie with a train behind you. Keep walking until you spot on the other side Putney Bridge station, the entrance for the Underground.

CHAPTER 8: ON THE SURFACE

No Man's Land at Southwark

Up until 1999, the Jubilee line only ran between Stanmore and Charing Cross where trains then terminated. But in the late 1990s the line was extended to what is now known as the JLE (the Jubilee line Extension). Nowadays, the line doesn't stop at Charing Cross but runs under the Thames, through Waterloo then beyond to Canary Wharf and eventually to Stratford in the east.

The Jubilee line has many interchange points with other lines. The one that is most intriguing is the connection at Southwark.

Finding No Man's Land

The main entrance, and most popular, is on the corner at the junction of The Cut and Blackfriars Road. When you come up the escalator to exit the station, instead of turning left to head for this entrance, you can turn right and follow the signs for Waterloo East. That's right, the Tube is so close to Waterloo East station that a walking route was put in place, and it leads to a rather intriguing no man's land which connects the Tube to the National Rail station.

Come up the stairs, or escalators, towards Waterloo East and exit through the barriers. You are now in no man's land. There is nothing to do here and nowhere else to go (i.e. there's no exit to the street). There are only more ticket barriers. Ten metres in front of you are the barriers that take you up to the National Railway station at Waterloo East.

If you've never been before, or made this interchange, it's a novel and fun place to go and stand for a moment to take in your surroundings then realise that you are stuck with nowhere else to go, except into another railway station.

From the Outside

There's one more bonus thing that you can do here. Observe this no man's land from the street outside. To do this, exit out of Southwark station the normal way, turn right, and walk along the main road of The Cut. After a minute, turn right again into the street called Hatfields.

A short way down here, on the left-hand side, you'll see a silver building and some windows which you can peer into. If you press your face up against the glass, you'll find yourself looking into that very same no man's land, but from the outside. The glass is here to let daylight into that area.

CHAPTER 8: ON THE SURFACE

Walk the Length of a Tube Line

Many people use the Tube map as the map to navigate their way around the city of London. However, despite the brilliance of Henry Beck's diagram, it can also be misleading. Some of the stations are shown in slightly different geographical positions than where they actually are.

So why not try to get a realistic sense of the stations by walking the entire length of the line. Looking at the map, you'll see that some of these are easier to do than others. There's certainly a very easy one, and some very difficult ones!

Waterloo & City Line Walk

The easiest is to walk between Waterloo and Bank for the Waterloo & City line. It takes thirty-five minutes at just over a mile and a half long. You can go via Southbank along the Thames, past the OXO Tower, cross over Blackfriars Bridge, and then walk up Queen Victoria Street through Mansion House, and into the City of London until you get to Bank.

Victoria Line Walk

An all-day challenge would be to walk the length of the Victoria line. It is timetabled as taking just over half an hour by Tube, thirty-one minutes from end to end. Up on the streets of London, if you

CHAPTER 8: ON THE SURFACE

followed the route above ground, it takes about four and a half hours to walk the fourteen miles.

Start at Brixton in the morning and head up Stockwell Road to Stockwell station. From here, head directly north to Vauxhall, and once you've ticked that off, cross over the Thames using Vauxhall Bridge and you'll get to Pimlico. Keep going up Vauxhall Bridge Road until you get to Victoria station itself. For the next part, you will walk past Buckingham Palace, and then the lovely Green Park to get to Green Park station.

Cut through the back streets of Mayfair, looking at the posh shops as you go. You'll get to Oxford Circus. Go through Fitzrovia to Warren Street, then along Euston Road to Euston, and then King's Cross.

Here, the Victoria line stations are a little further apart. It is one of the longest distances between two stations. Walk through the back streets, cross the Regent's Canal and come up to Upper Street to get to Highbury & Islington. Pass the Arsenal Emirates football stadium to get to Finsbury Park, and then you're on to the final stretch.

Go directly past Finsbury Park (the Piccadilly line is also beneath your feet at this point) and then north-east up Seven Sisters Road to get to Seven Sisters Tube station. Along and around Broad Lane to get to Tottenham Hale, then between the huge reservoirs via Ferry Lane and Forest Road to get to Blackhorse Road. Then for the final section, head south-east through the side roads to get to Walthamstow and have a well-earned rest with some food and drink!

Obviously take a picture outside each station as you go, with the sign clearly visible in the background so you can say that you've walked the entire length of the Victoria line.

CHAPTER 9

JUST FOR FUN

CHAPTER 9: JUST FOR FUN

The Victoria Line's Amazing Tile Patterns

Have you ever noticed, when travelling on the Victoria line, that each of the sixteen stations uses different tiled motifs on the platform walls? These are in the area where the seats are recessed.

When the line was built in 1969, prominent artists and designers were commissioned to create designs which related to the name of the station, or the history of its surrounding area. Those are the designs that you see today along the length of the light blue line.

The sixteen tile pattern designs that you can see are:

Walthamstow: this is an adaption of a design by artist William Morris who was born in Walthamstow.

Blackhorse Road: here you'll see a black horse. There's one outside the station on the side of the station building as well.

Tottenham Hale: the name is derived from a small ferry that crossed over the River Lea in earlier times and is shown here.

🔹 **Seven Sisters:** the tiles show the seven trees which gave the name to this station.

🔹 **Finsbury Park:** the crossed pistols refer to the duelling that used to take place here.

🔹 **Highbury & Islington:** the tiles show the high bury, manor, or castle that was destroyed at the time of the Peasants' Revolt in 1381.

🔹 **King's Cross St Pancras:** a literal design based on a cross and crowns.

🔹 **Euston:** a reminder of the Doric arch which once stood at the original grand entrance to the station.

🔹 **Warren Street:** a maze, or warren, as a pun on the name; solve it while you wait for the train.

🔹 **Oxford Circus:** a simple design that incorporates the circle which links up the Bakerloo, Central, and Victoria lines.

🔹 **Green Park:** this was once a bird's-eye view of the trees in the park against the green background of the grass, but the motif was replaced in 1979 with a leaf design by June Fraser to match the new Jubilee line platforms.

Victoria: the great Queen herself, from a silhouette.

Pimlico: the spots represent modern art at the nearby Tate Britain gallery.

Vauxhall: the nice design here is a visual representation of the old Vauxhall Pleasure Gardens.

Stockwell: this is a picture of a swan. Look closely and you can see the orange beak. There is pub across the road from the station called The Swan.

Brixton: designed by Hans Unger, the picture of the red bricks is a simple pun on the station's name. A Ton of Bricks is Brixton.

Bonus! There's also another seated recess of plain coloured tiles (no pattern) at Old Street station on the Northern line. It's the same style and design but just with plain coloured tiles. For the perfectionist in you, pop along and snap a picture of that too.

CHAPTER 9: JUST FOR FUN

Under the River Thames

Which Tube line crosses to River Thames the most? Quick! Can you come up with an answer without looking at the map?

The Tube crosses the Thames (either under in a tunnel, or over on a bridge) in ten places: twice on the District line (between Kew Gardens and Gunnersbury, and Putney Bridge and East Putney), on the Bakerloo line (between Waterloo and Embankment), on the Victoria line (between Vauxhall and Pimlico), twice on the Northern line (between Waterloo and Embankment, and London Bridge and Bank), as well as the Waterloo & City line (between Waterloo and Bank). But the winner is the Jubilee line, which crosses under the Thames four times in total. Three of them are so close together that you can do it in under five minutes.

How to Do it

Start at Canada Water on the Jubilee line and take an eastbound train towards Stratford. You will immediately be travelling underneath the Thames, and will continue to do so before reaching Canary Wharf ninety seconds later.

Due to the bend in the river in the Docklands area, you will again pass under the Thames as you travel between Canary Wharf and North Greenwich.

Up above, the river has turned again, while down below the

Jubilee is also making a turn to the north, which means that the Underground passes beneath the river again.

All of this should be five minutes as you travel between North Greenwich and come out into the open again at Canning Town.

What was your time? Did you manage to go under the Thames three times in five minutes?

The Tube's Longest Journey

The longest possible single journey that you can take on one train is on the Central line between West Ruislip and Epping (or vice versa) at the length of thirty-four miles.

Start out in Zone 6 in West London. If you make this journey you will pass through thirty-eight stations. That's 78% of the Central line's forty-nine stations in one big swoop! According to the timetables, it should take one hour and twenty-three minutes to complete. That's if you stay on the train, which you could do one way and then on the way back there are plenty of interesting spots you can stop off to visit.

CHAPTER 9: JUST FOR FUN

Top Four Places to See Along the Central Line

● Buckhurst Hill

When Buckhurst Hill was first built in 1856, before it was part of the London Underground, this station was once located on Queen's Road. Later, in 1892, the station entrance was moved to where it is now, but if you take a short walk, or use the new step-free entrance at the south end of the platforms, you can spot the original station building!

● St Paul's

When you exit this station, the ticket hall is beneath the street, and you come up to the exit or entrance using the escalators. However, when the station was originally built the entrance and exit wasn't there. So where was it? Walk west, down towards Newgate Street, and you'll see a triangular traffic island right by Christchurch Tower. You will also see a dark-brick, nondescript building, and note that there are signs on the

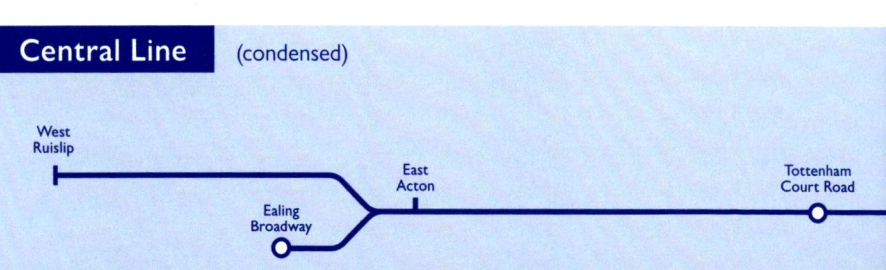

door which use the Johnston font. This is because this space acts as a ventilation shaft down to the Tube below, which is still used! This is also where the original entrance was located when it had lifts. It was moved so that escalators could be installed at the station.

 East Acton

Get out at East Acton and walk down Du Cane Road towards Hammersmith Hospital. Almost opposite the entrance, by the zebra crossing, is a small alleyway which takes you to a footbridge that goes over an above-ground section of the Central line. What's interesting to see here is the point at which the tracks cross over (after being the wrong way around at White City). So here the tracks are on the correct, left-hand side again. Stay and see if you can get a photo of two trains crossing over each other!

West Ruislip

At the end of the line itself, you can see how it almost wasn't the end of the line. Outside the front of the station, cross over the road and peer over the bridge onto the tracks below. You can see, to the right, the mainline for Chiltern Trains that travels along here. You can also see that the Central line track carries on for a short section where the line had been proposed to extend to Denham, but was never built.

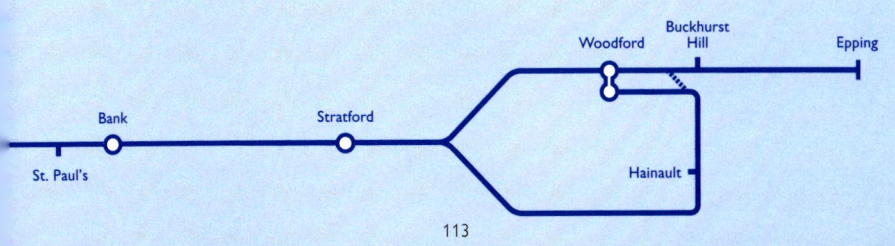

CHAPTER 10

TUBE CHALLENGES

CHAPTER 10: TUBE CHALLENGES

The Tube Challenge (as it's commonly known) is a challenge in which you must travel to all Underground stations on the network in one day. This was first recorded in 1959 and has been tried by many people since. It is something that is often listed in the Guinness Book of Records. If you are the fastest, you can have a World Record Certificate for this.

The aim of the challenge is to stop at every station in the fastest time possible while following a few simple rules. You don't have to get out, or leave the station (the train just has to stop). You may only go on foot (walking or running) or use scheduled forms of public transport (e.g. other trains and buses) to make connections. Having a lift in a car, taking a taxi, or even riding a bike (including cycle hire schemes) are strictly against the rules.

Doing this challenge takes all day (somewhere in the region of eighteen hours) and is therefore extremely demanding and tiring. This is why smaller Tube challenges have sprung up. They take less time, and are easier to complete. They all adhere to the same basic rules though: you must only use public transport to stop at (and not pass through) the stations on the challenge. Here then are some alternative challenges which you can do if you're not up for doing the whole thing.

CHAPTER 10: TUBE CHALLENGES

 ## All Tube Lines Challenge

We'll start with one of my favourites, arguably the most fun and quickest challenge to complete. The name is a little deceptive as it doesn't mean that you must cover all the lines, but rather just one part of every line in the quickest time possible. You must ride at least one stop (or more) on each of the eleven Tube lines. This can be done in under an hour.

 ## All Rail Lines Challenge

If you think covering all the Tube lines sounds easy, then the ultimate challenge takes it one step further. You must include the London Overground, Trams, DLR, TfL Rail, and even the Cable Car, which is shown on the Tube map. That's sixteen different lines that you can try to travel in the quickest way possible!

 ## The Park Challenge

You don't have to visit any parks to complete this challenge (but if you were doing it in the summer and it was a nice day, then perhaps you could), instead simply visit all twenty-four stations on the map that have the word 'park' in their name. Take a photo of yourself in front of a roundel at each station, and then hop back on again. This will most likely take between eight and nine hours to do, so allow a little longer for comfort breaks and time to eat.

CHAPTER 10: TUBE CHALLENGES

To complete this challenge, you will be making your way from Moor Park on the Metropolitan to Elm Park on the District. Here's the list of those twenty-four stations that you need to visit.

Belsize Park, Canons Park, Chiswick Park, Elm Park, Finsbury Park, Green Park, Holland Park, Hyde Park Corner, Kilburn Park, Moor Park, Newbury Park, Northwick Park, Park Royal, Queen's Park, Regent's Park, Ravenscourt Park, St James's Park, Stonebridge Park, Tufnell Park, Upton Park, Westbourne Park, Wembley Park, Wimbledon Park, Woodside Park

45 Royal Challenge

Similar to the park challenge, there are seventeen stations that have the words 'Royal', 'King', or 'Queen' in their name. You could include the DLR as well, which adds Royal Victoria, Prince Regent, Royal Albert, and King George V to the list of stations, taking it to twenty-two in total. Otherwise the list is as follows:

Barking, Barkingside, Dalston Kingsland, King's Cross St Pancras, King George V, Kingsbury, Park Royal, Prince Regent, Queen's Park, Queens Road Peckham, Queensbury, Queensway, Royal Albert, Royal Oak, Royal Victoria, Victoria, Walthamstow Queen's Road.

CHAPTER 10: TUBE CHALLENGES

 ## 46 The Circle Line Challenge

There's something quite satisfying about being able to say you've visited all the stations that fall within the Circle line. The best part of it is that there are only forty-eight stations in total. It should be possible in under three hours.

You have to travel to every station on the Circle line, plus all the stations that fall inside the circle on the map. On current Tube maps, the Bakerloo line at Marylebone and Edgware Road appear outside of the Circle line, so you won't have to do these two stops. But it's worth noting that over the years the design of the map has changed, so you may come across older designs where these stations were once inside the Circle line. As modern-day maps have them outside, we say don't do them.

 ## 47 Visit All 272 Stations Over a Year

Here's a brilliant one which we've challenged people to do on our YouTube channel. If you're going to do this one, it helps to start early in the year. You could plan it so that you start on 1 January and finish it bang on 31 December in the same year!

The challenge is to say that you've got on or off at, and been outside of, every Tube station on the network. That's all 272 of them! Maybe take a picture of yourself outside of each one with the name of the station in the background.

CHAPTER 10: TUBE CHALLENGES

We know that this challenge means a fair bit of travelling (and fares) over a few days, so the most efficient way of doing it is to set aside a couple of days a month (the weekends and public holidays are good as the fares are off-peak all day) and visit several stations in one day. If you hit the cap on your Oyster card, then it might be worth doing a few more to make the most of your fares for that day.

The stations in Zone 1 are probably the easiest to do because some of them are possible to walk between. You can search online for the excellent 'walking Tube map' to show you which stations are walkable. The trickier ones are in the higher zones. The Woodford to Hainault trains only run once every twenty minutes, for example, and the Metropolitan line train at Amersham and Chesham can run only once every half an hour, so not as frequent as every two to three minutes in the middle of London.

48 The Zone 1 Challenge: Visit All 64 Stations in Zone 1

Here's an easier version of the all stations challenge. Can you visit just sixty-four stations that are in the Zone 1 area on the Tube map?

Take the challenge that you would do for the Circle line challenge and expand it to the rest of the stations in Zone 1. At the top of Zone 1 are Paddington, Edgware Road, and Marylebone on the Bakerloo line. The bottom of Zone 1 stretches out beyond the Circle line to include Pimlico and Vauxhall on the Victoria line, Elephant & Castle and Lambeth North on the Bakerloo line, Waterloo, Southwark, and London Bridge on the Jubilee line, and then Borough on the Northern line.

CHAPTER 10: TUBE CHALLENGES

49   Visit All 272 Stations in a Day

Our penultimate challenge has been saved until here for a reason. It's the ultimate and biggest challenge that you can undertake on the Tube. It is to visit all the stations on the Underground in one day. At the time of writing, the current fastest time (for 272 stations) is seventeen hours, forty-six minutes, and forty-eight seconds.

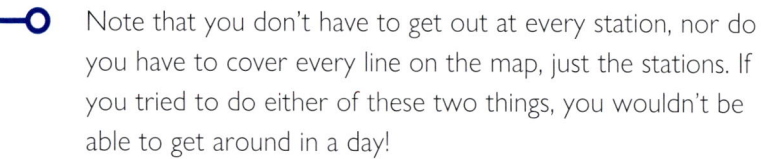

Top Tips

To do this challenge, you must be on a train that stops at every station. Currently that's 272 stations, which now includes the two new stations on the Northern line extension at Nine Elms and Battersea Power Station.

- Note that you don't have to get out at every station, nor do you have to cover every line on the map, just the stations. If you tried to do either of these two things, you wouldn't be able to get around in a day!

- Typically, your day has to start early, around 6 a.m., and then you finish as fast as you can. In our experience it is usually around 11 p.m.

- A good amount of planning for a swift route is essential. It's also almost essential to start or finish any route you do in the north-west corner of the map at either Amersham or Chesham.

CHAPTER 10: TUBE CHALLENGES

- There are three tricky sections of the Tube which many will find awkward: the first is Mill Hill East on the Northern line where the trains run only run every fifteen minutes; the Woodford to Hainault section of the Central line, where trains are only every twenty minutes; and then the hardest station of all of is Kensington (Olympia), which only gets a few trains in the morning, and then two trains in the evening.

- People often ask if you can use the London Overground to tick off Olympia, but this doesn't count as the official rules state that it must be done using the Underground. However, it's perfectly acceptable to arrive at Olympia on a District line train from Earls Court, then change and leave on an Overground train which heads south down to West Brompton where you can pick up the District line again.

- To make connections between stations at the end (or near end) of lines, buses can be used. The 307 bus between Oakwood and High Barnet is often used. You can use a bus between Wimbledon on the District line and South Wimbledon on the Northern line.

- Connections that can be done on foot (at running speed if you like) are Kenton (Bakerloo line) to Northwick Park (Metropolitan line), and West Ruislip (Central line) to Ickenham (Piccadilly/Metropolitan line). There are many other connections and different ways to do them, but half the fun of these challenges is studying a map, as well as a street map of London, and figuring them all out yourself.

CHAPTER 11

LONDON'S NEWEST RAILWAY